STREETWISE

STREETWISE

The Alternative Motorcycle Survival Manual

MALCOLM NEWELL

**Illustrations by
PAUL SAMPLE**

First Published in 1989 by Osprey Publishing Limited
59 Grosvenor Street
London WIX 9DA

British Library Cataloguing in Publication Data
Newell, Malcolm
Streetwise
1. Motorcycling
I. Title
796.7

ISBN 0-85045-824-2

Editor Nicholas Collins
Design Simon Bell

Typeset by BookEns, Saffron Walden, Essex
Printed in Great Britain by J. W. Arrowsmith Ltd., Bristol

CONTENTS

PREFACE

This manual deals with what is average, normal or most likely to occur, so, it *does* contain some sweeping generalisations, e.g. 'Women are not only different in the biological sense but also have a different mental outlook, an outlook which is very noticeable in their driving.'

You may know of, or even be that female who has the endearing male attributes in full – aggression, egocentricity, impatience – and could run rings round us all. We would not doubt you but for the sake of clarity these exceptional people and happenings are hereby put to one side to concentrate on the norm.

WELCOME

Welcome to 'Streetwise', the alternative riding manual for the motorcycle, that cost-effective freedom machine that releases you from the timetables of public transport and the harrassments of hold ups, parking and expense to which the average car driver is subject. You can now travel faster than a Ferrari for less than a tenth of the cost, ride up Ben Nevis, visit your Gran or see Tibet. Motorcyling is poetry in motion. It can certainly warp time and mind, produce a great adrenaline buzz, put more smiles on your dial per mile, and satisfy the soul.

BUT there is a high risk factor. Death and deformity cannot be discounted. However, as the miles and years pass by, experience gained reduces the risks; surviving the errors increases your knowledge. If error is the price of skill we, the survivors, would like to help the novice to achieve maturity.

So we asked for the experiences of bikers with ten years or more of riding what they had learnt that should be included in this guide. From venerables and veterans, couriers and constables the information came in. It's synthesised and condensed but it's all here – experience which we hope will be of use to you in your years to come.

I

FIRST HASSLES

Your first hassle will probably occur in the acquisition of your mount. Unlike the purchase of a car, a motorcycle is unlikely to get the full-hearted approval of your parents, and they can be most adamant in their objections, fearing that their darling offspring is likely to top him or herself. If you are the eldest or only offspring, you will be taking the brunt and blame for being a deviant in the normal nuclear family. The persuasion necessary to move your kin to a more enlightened way of thinking will probably have to be two-tiered. The practical values will probably appeal to your pater. He knows a bike will cost a lost less in outlay and running costs than a second or third car in the family. It will take up less room and you will not have an excuse for borrowing his car or asking him to chauffeur you around.

Besides, it shows that you have all the right balance of chromozomes for a normal healthy male – undoubtedly a hereditary gift from him.

Emotion is a more likely line of appeal to mater – without a bike your growth may be stunted, your mind deviated towards drugs and anti-social habits and your career prospects restricted by a lack of transport to get to higher centres of learning or up-market job opportunities. Besides, it's a very small bike that you're proposing to buy, limited by the law to speeds slower than a push bike, and with the training you are going to get from eminent persons on bike training schemes you will come to no permanent harm.

Your parents are not likely to believe all you say, but by

persevering and accepting that they are trying in their negative way to protect you from danger, you should be able to get them to see by stages that this is just another step on the road to maturity for you.

Go easy on the heavy verbals – you may need a loan or a signature for the HP form. It's no good having wrung consent from them to find yourself thwarted by a lack of readies.

Assuming the negotiations have gone satisfactorily, where is the machine to be acquired? In the previous parental fracas you may have been down to your local training centre to enlist aid in placating your parents' anxiety. This time ask them if there are any machines available, or likely to be, from the intake who have recently passed or are about to take the test.

Or look in newsagents' windows for ads before purchasing that grand old comic, *Motor Cycle News* or your local *Motor Trader*. Next, stop at the dealers acting as agents for one of the major manufacturers. Ask them what they would recommend as the best model to purchase, past or present, and what is wrong with the opposition. Without doubt they will praise their own bikes and criticise the other makes but from these prejudiced viewpoints you should still get some useful information.

Showroom prices are always high compared to private

purchase from an individual but dealerships do offer the convenience of HP. It is robbery without violence and dealers love it. Apart from not giving a cash or trade in discount, they will twist your arm to load on insurance and clothing. Signing up is easy: paying back becomes harder with the passing months as the first pride of ownership becomes tempered with the thought that all the purchases are at least 25 per cent more expensive because of interest charges.

Remember with HP, you have three days to change your mind after signing the agreement. However, before signing you should look to see how much interest you will be paying. Be aware, too, that if you fall behind with repayments they can come and take the bike away (unless you have paid a third of it – then they will have to get a Court Order first). The good news is that if you are flush enough at any time to pay off the whole balance outstanding you can, under the terms of the Consumer Credit Act 1974, see if you can get some of that interest knocked off. HP is different from other means of purchasing in that the goods are not legally yours until the last instalment has been paid.

You will notice that if, within a few miles you ask the dealer to repurchase the bike, his enthusiasm will have diminished considerably and he will buy back the as-new bike at about 25 per cent less than you paid for it!

It is cheaper, if possible, to borrow the money from the family

or failing that from your local friendly bank manager. The interest you will have to pay out on an overdraft or a personal loan will probably be cheaper than with an HP agreement and at least the machine is legally yours – nobody is going to come and snatch-back the bike, although you may well get letters from the bank reminding you that your overdraft or loan remains unpaid. With cash in hand you might also be able to argue a discount from the dealer, too.

In any event, do not hurry. Give yourself a month, in which time you will have found your sources of finance, list of makes and models in order of preference, their likely prices and insurance quotes. If you are buying second-hand, find out the prices of replacement parts such as tyres, chains, sprockets and pads. A bargain may eventually cost you more if it has been neglected or abused than the going rate for a well maintained example.

Most of us lose the ability to be objective when confronted with the object of our desires. This ability to fool ourselves reduces the necessity for salesmanship on the part of those that are doing the selling. So do not rush it, keep cool and take along a friend who knows more than you do about motorcycle mechanics. If the machine does not sound how you think a bike should – back off. If the seller does not have the paperwork to hand (i.e. log book with matching numbers to those on the frame/engine plus MOT if relevant) – back off. If there is anything mechanical or personal that sticks in your craw – back off. It's better to have lost a bargain than gained a lemon with the associated chance of financial ruin.

The choice of bike is limited not only by what you can afford, but also by governmental decree to a 50cc, 35 mph maximum moped at the age of 16. Machines built before August 1977 are not restricted and could keep up with the normal urban traffic flow. Most of these mopeds are knackered by now but depending on the make and model you may be able to resuscitate one for a price.

At age 17 you can get a motor bike with a maximum capacity of 125 cc and 12 bhp. Models before 1982 were not nobbled by legislation. This has not as yet screwed up your right to have an 'outfit', alias a motorcycle and sidecar. There is no restriction on cubic capacity or power for a learner driving one of these and you can carry unqualified, unhelmeted passengers legally in the chair and you do not have to take a Part One test. The insurance is also lower in price than an equivalent solo but the riding technique demanded is like no other. Although you have normal bike controls, the results of having a sidecar attached makes the handling anything but normal.

Motorcyclists are an easy target for the police and civil servants to harrass with draconian laws as the majority of the

population do not want to be involved in anything adventurous and there is little support for those who do. This leads the law-makers to produce even more restrictive laws at the expense of the motorcyclists civil liberties. So join the Motorcycle Action Group (MAG) and British Motorcycle Federation (BMF), become politically aware and articulate and stop them before they take away your right to be alive to life.

A full car licence acts as a provisional licence for bikes and as a full licence for mopeds. At this time you are not legally required to take a bike test and may stay on a provisional licence indefinitely. Without a full car licence, you will need to apply for a provisional driving licence with motorcycle entitlement (form D from Post Offices). This costs £10 and is valid for just two years. If you do not take and pass both parts of the driving test in those two years, you will be banned for the next 12 months.

Remember that if you fail, you go to the end of a long waiting list monitored by civil servants who are never in any hurry to pick your name out of the hat. Two years is not that long when

the system is against you, so get to it, and apply for your test sooner rather than later. If possible keep your moped as the licence entitles you to continue to ride it even though you are not allowed to ride a bike for twelve months. At least it's personal mobility.

Documents now in your possession should include the log book (alias Vehicle Registration Document (VRD)). If your bike was bought second-hand the previous owner would have kept the bottom section and you would have sent off the rest, having filled in the relevant spaces on the back of the top section to the Driver & Vehicle Licencing Centre (DVLC for short) at Swansea, SA99 IAR. After a time, a new VRD in your name will have been forwarded to you.

And if your bike is over three years old, a MOT certificate will have to be obtained. These can be had from those motor cycle establishments which display a large blue sign with three triangles – two above and one below in white. As the cost is high for the service you get, it's best not to receive a failure sheet. Have a go at checking over and adjusting or replacing the worn components yourself. Things such as brake pads, chain and bulbs only need a degree of commonsense to rectify.

Put the bike on its centre stand and place something heavy on the back to raise the front wheel clear of the ground. Then, standing at the front of the bike, pull the wheel spindle towards you. If it moves, check and tighten the head-set and check that it still turns freely. If the wheel and fork self-centres, you have a notched head race which will need replacing. Spin the wheel, see that it's running true and check that the brake stops it rotating.

Do not forget to pull the wheel sideways towards a fork leg to check for loose wheel bearings. All the spokes should be tightly in position. Tyres have to have at least 2 mm of tread and no breaks or abrasions. Check brake pads or shoes for the amount of lining left and adjust if necessary. The same pro-cedures also apply to the real wheel where a sideways pull is also necessary to check for swing arm wear. Sprockets, chain and cables should also be tested for wear and adjustment.

Electrical components are critically important, so make sure that there are none missing, and those that are there actually work. Check indicators, horn, brake lights, head and dip. Make sure the exhaust is not noisy or leaking and everything else is secure and sound. A fuel tank held on with baler twine and broken mudguard stays are points to look out for.

If you are in doubt about the standard of your bike, some of the better dealers will, for a few notes, do you a pre-MOT check, so you know for certain what needs doing.

After three years' use from new, the machine will require an MOT certificate when you come to get a 'vehicle licence' – generally known as road tax. This expensive piece of paper should be mounted in a holder somewhere on the left, or near side, of the bike and in front of the steering head.

Another problem can be posed by 'L' plates. These are normally flimsy bits of plastic that have to be mounted on a flat surface facing to the front and rear. Flat surfaces are in short supply on motorcycles, so you will have to improvise, if the previous owner or dealer has not already done so. The rear is quite easy. Make up a length of hardboard, ply or alloy, with the depth and width the same dimensions as the rear number plate and 'L' plate combined. Sandwich it between the number plate mount and the number plate. (You may have to use longer bolts.) Stick the 'L' plate onto the bit left sticking out.

The front takes a bit more work to get to the mounting points. You can use the top or bottom fork yoke pinch bolts – or perhaps the flyscreen, headlight or indicator attachment bolts. Do not tie, tape or stick it to anything else other than those legally required flat surfaces because it gives the police one more reason to cause you wallet fatigue if it is not done right.

An insurance certificate for Third Party makes you road legal but it will only cover you for causing injury or death to another person, or damage to their property, but nowt for you. Third Party Fire & Theft (TPFT) is not dissimilar but it does help you if your machine is stolen or catches fire. Comprehensive insurance is at least as twice as expensive as TPFT but it gives reimbursement for damage to yourself and your machine and clothing, no matter who is to blame. However, all claims put your No Claims Bonus in jeopardy. This is a form of incentive

not to claim for minor damage as it is sometimes possible to get up to 40 per cent discount, for example, after five clear years, which might represent an awful lot more in value than a broken indicator lens or scratched tank.

Insurance companies are not there as an altruistic public service. They are there to make as much money as possible with the least risk to themselves. You will not be received with open arms or a happy smile, because their statistics tell them that motorcyclists cause them to unclamp their purses and pay out more frequently than their other motoring clients. So, should you have to claim, they will try to connive and blind you with the small print and take longer and give a lot less than you expected when they finally do pay up. Any claim, no matter whose fault or what policy you paid for will make you *persona non grata* and even more if the Courts add points to your licence. You are going to have to pay even more for your insurance if drinking and driving is involved – at least a 100 per cent increase in your subscription. Even a refusal to quote you for insurance could be on the cards.

2

CLOTHING

Clothing not only holds the naughty parts in and away from view but it is also a sign of your rank, status and mood. It can keep you warm, dry and protected and cause you to be welcomed or rejected.

Being a biker will probably mean you will be spending a lot of time in, and money on, apparel that will not be welcomed by your average punter. In fact, you will be discriminated against. These prejudices normally come from middle class pretensions of conformity and dislike of the unconforming minority of which you are now a member.

When suiting up to do battle with the elements and your Sunday-only Christian passes by with that look of revulsion, it is not you personally but your raiment that causes the problem, and as no explanation or reasonable dialogue will penetrate such fixed conceptions, ignore the twat. Compromise not your safety on the altar of respectability.

Bone domes, crash hats, lids, brain buckets or helmets should be your first acquisition because (a) it's the law, (b) it will please your elders, (c) it will help save your skull from being cracked by the street or truncheons and (d) it stops your hair from getting wet.

There are three basic styles – full face, open face and pudding bowl. The first offers the greatest amount of protection because it normally incorporates a moveable visor and a chin guard, giving a wider range of vision than goggles. It is also less likely to wear your chin away while travelling face down getting a closer look at the tarmac. The drawbacks are that it is difficult to talk when wearing one. The visors also mist up and can become easily scratched when removing bugs and road spray, something which makes night driving even more difficult. Full face, when not on your bonce, can serve as a bum perch, hand bag or ale carrier.

With the open face helmet, you can have a conver-

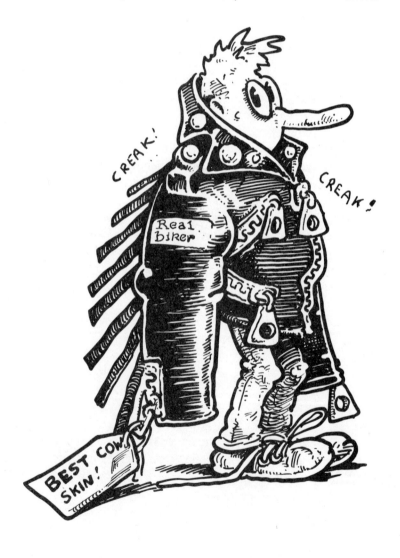

sation without having to remove it, and wear goggles which do not mist up so easily. Laminated glass lenses also have the advantage of lasting at least ten times as long without vision deterioration than plastic goggles or visors.

Pudding bowls are for yesterday's man, in keeping with yesterday's bike; they trigger nostalgia quicker than a leather flying cap.

Black leather jackets are a very popular item of apparel but not as useful as waxed cotton Barbours or Belstaffs. However, they have better abrasion resistance when visiting the tarmac and a greater sex appeal and style than the waxed cotton's utilitarian approach. They lose out, however, when it rains. Waxed cotton may not be elegant but it will keep you warm and dry and those pockets could carry a spare bike! Nylon and plastic oversuits and trousers are ideal for keeping your leathers dry, but do not expect anything else for your money. Boots: for that Third Reich look they should be calf length with back or side zip, or if you are so inclined, Moto cross with wonderous colours and mega buckles. Failing either, get a pair of ex-WD boots or Docs laced up to the ankle. All these give support and pinky protection, even when kick starting that 500 single.

In the glove department the choice is wide, ranging from gauntlets to string backs. Their prime purpose is to delay the onset of frostbite or drowned digits. Moto cross versions have built in knuckle protectors and boy racer gloves incorporate a chamois leather visor wiper; tourers favour a glove with an overmitt in a little pouch on the back.

One-piece tailor-made leathers with body amour are the utlimate in price and poseur value and safety. Looks good on the GPZ but a bit OTT on that step-through AND you will need a change of clothes with you if you want to do anything but biking. The zip-up two-piece is somewhat better because you can partially disrobe; the top when hot and hectic and the bottom when the rectum is suffering and needs to be quickly parked on the nearest porcelain.

The need for concentration is never greater than when the weather is inclement, so if your body is bitching about the rigours you are subjecting it to, the brain will not be able to sustain reasonable reaction times.

3

TRAINING

This will involve the necessity of your conforming to a uniform standard of blind obedience, with a 'Do as I say' attitude from the trainers. As you need to get a licence, you will have to obey – and also pay a lot of money as the Part I training and test is in the hands of private enterprise; more dedicated to money than service.

The Part I test as such is likely in the next year or two to be replaced by even more draconian legislation, as the Pursuit Part 2 test is brought into being. Pursuit Part 2 is going to be more expensive, take longer and be much easier to fail. As you would expect, Testers are chosen for and schooled in surly and hostile behaviour designed to intimidate. The only time they seem pleased is when they fail you. The majority of Bike Testers have only ridden a bike for six weeks or less (presumably to get on a higher salary scale while also inflicting themselves on more than just car learner drivers). At least with motorcycles Bike Testers must put some effort into earning their wages through having to get out on the streets on a bike in all weathers. Just like you and me!

It is not going to make them any nicer, but decent training might dent that smug, self-satisfied attitude.

To have even a fifty per cent chance of passing your test you too will need training, but it will have to be at a higher level than is presently imposed. As it will still be in the hands of the private sector, your financial outlay could be crippling. Remember, they are doing it for profit and the government is doing it to stop you being a biker by putting as much hassle as it can possibly get away with between you and the pleasure and convenience of this mode of transport.

Our survey showed a very much lower pass rate on the Part 2 test for riders of bikes fitted with a leaning non-passenger carrying sidecar called a Sidewinder. This neat and practical product was brought about by the legislation curtailing the then learner limit of 250 cc, bringing it down to 125 cc, 12 bhp. This forced riders into financial hardship not of their making by making them sell a machine for which the market had dried up, and purchase one that was in greater demand. In comparison, this wondrous leaning chair at a fraction of the cost and without having to dispose of your current bike, enabled you legally to get back on the streets. Some test examiners see this as an attitude problem on your part and take umbridge, with no quarter given. You will have to do better than the best and even then you might fail. Another good idea screwed up by prejudiced bureaucracy.

4

STREET CONDITIONS

Country lanes running between high banks, stone walls and hedges are not reknowned as venues for biker fatalities, but you could still find yourself in intensive care.

These lanes seldom have kerbs, so the verges and banks leach soil onto the tarmac, reducing grip and stability for the bike. It is not too good for cars either because as the nearside wheels fail to grip, the offside wheels, usually on a better surface, can cause the car under braking to slew across the lane. Lanes show up how very insensitive the average driver's assimilation abilities and reaction times are. The may be slow on the B roads but they certainly drive too fast for the lanes.

Be thankful that there is normally enough space to squeeze through a solo bike if nobody panics. Pity the poor sidecar rider! If the car manages to miss him, he has still got to convince the pillock in charge that it is easier to reverse the car than push the chair backwards.

Estates Housing or industrial estates are usually enclaves of streets serving their own residents. Traffic is slow moving and less likely to use signals before manoeuvering. This is either because car drivers are busy trying to dicipher the map and find their directions, or they have lived at Dunroaming for the last millenium and have forgotten how to give signals. Pedestrians also exhibit less caution outside their own front door, especially the under-10s and over-60s. Pedestrians, together with canine and feline members of the community – strays or beloved family pets – all show a remarkable lack of respect for self-preservation.

You will quite likely find congestion on estates on a Sunday. Many of them contain shopping centres with their associated pool of inept Sunday drivers.

Towns Pedestrians *en masse* and tin tops in profusion both like queueing; the former at venues such as bus stops and toilets, so making it inevitable that some of the more mobile will step into the street to avoid the throng. If they are walking in the same direction as the traffic flow, there is little doubt that they will not have looked over their shoulder to check that they are not about to be shafted by the front wheel of a traffic-filtering bike.

Prams, baby buggies and invalid chairs may suddenly appear from between vehicles and around blind corners and in front of parked buses with the sole object of checking your reflexes. The idea of pulling a pram

rather than pushing it does not appear to be popular. It is the pedestrian pulling the pram who should first take the risk when crossing a road. The pedestrian can get out of the way much quicker than a pram can.

Parked cars need to be visually checked for occupants. It is people that are the real hazard. Has the car just parked? Then it is likely that the door or doors will be flung ajar without first checking mirrors. Is the driver just about to vacate that parking space? Then it will probably be the whole car and not just a door that will be an impediment to your progress.

Delivery vehicles try to park as close to their drop as

possible, even if it means illegal parking. They normally put on hazard flashers, but if another lorry masks the hazard nearside flasher, it can appear as if the vehicle is signalling its intent to get back into the traffic flow. Some of the more cautious drivers – or those who think they have at last found a chance to park – wait for this vehicle to pull out, but as there is four tons to shift, papers to check and cheques to be handed over, and it's time for a bevvy anyway, there is no chance of vacant possession for at least a quarter of an hour. You will find it will not take that long for a general raising of tempers and a lowering of driving standards in the vicinity.

Urban riding is the most hazardous to health for the motorcyclist. It takes many years to get the degree of experience to enable the motorcyclist to keep out of the casualty ward or burial casket. Those that survive, like despatch riders, are the very best practitioners of the art of urban survival.

B roads There are more B roads than any other class of blacktop in Britain and they are by far the nicest for getting the best out of bike and rider. They carry enough traffic for them to be well maintained and signposted with the better class of hazard, chevron or a pictorial warning displayed (but not enough to seriously impede your progress). And motorcyclists get a lot less hassle and harrassment from the 'Blue Meanies,' and are also more likely to find a good welcome at the inn of their choice on these less-frequented roads.

Dual and A roads These were the most important highways, before the advent of motorways. Before and after the Second World War by-passes and dual carriageways were built to speed up the traffic flow whilst trying to reduce the delays and damage that such building involves.

This process has continued in a haphazard fashion to the present day, in some cases providing a fair imitation of a motorway. They are handy if you are on 'L' plates to practise and assimilate motorway-style hazards and problems. On a few of them you can still find those old fashioned truckers' cafes. These hostelries – low on etiquette: high in value – are the opposite of those plastic palaces whose hostile service to bikers and miniscule portions are to be avoided if you do not want to put a large dent in your drinking vouchers.

Motorways On motorways the speed of the traffic is much higher than on A roads or even dual carriageways, so the lower-powered bikes will find themselves travelling on the inside lane, overtaking and being overtaken by the heavy brigade. Over the years the inside lane, especially on the older motorways, has had its surface rippled and cracked on the upgrades by the commercials. On the downgrades, the motorcyclist has to contend with tarmac impregnated with diesel and oil, plus the hazards of shed treads, blown carcasses, coiled ropes and blocks of wood.

The other exciting factor that the heavy brigade has to offer is the effect of their airflow; the bigger the truck, the bigger the turbulance. The greater the speed differential the more you will find its presence felt if you have not been concentrating on your riding. By the time you hear the noise you will be hit by the pressure wave of the front of the cab pushing you out onto the hard shoulder; then it will suck you back as you are picked up by the laminar flow down the side of the body, and pulled very close to the truck. If it is really loaded you will feel the road actually shaking under you. On top of this there is the noise of the engine transmission and tyres. But it is not over yet – there is the tail vortex. This is caused by large flat backs producing a low pressure area which sucks in the surrounding turbulent air and buffets the motorcycle as it passes. If there are a number of trucks in convoy this will leave you very little time to recover your equilibrium before being consumed yet again! And that is on a good day. On a bad one, in the fog, wind, snow and freezing conditions, you will probably wonder about your sanity. You

can reduce some of the apprehension by not being taken by surprise and having some idea what is going to happen and why.

Using a section of the hard shoulder in bad conditions can help. Gently change track and when it's clear, do the same on the return. However, there is likely to be some stationary vehicles and a lot of gravel and debris on the hard shoulder. If in

doubt, park as far onto the shoulder as possible and wait until matters improve. Get up to a reasonable speed – if possible the same as the traffic you are about to join – and slot neatly into a gap.

Travelling faster than the flow of traffic you face similar problems, but the solutions are different. Coming up behind a truck you will notice an increase in the bike's performance, especially if it masks you from a head wind and you pick up its suction. You can wind some throttle off and still travel at the same speed but should you decide to overtake, go out as far as you can without changing lanes and if the truck masks you from a cross wind, be prepared for a course alteration. It can be helpful when about to exit the wind break, if you have not committed to the passing manoeuvre, to tweak the throttle as you pass back into that side pressure. This has the effect of taking up any chassis slack and momentarily increasing tyre loads through an increase in aerodynamic pressure. You can also lay on the the tank to reduce drag, decrease side pressure, and increase velocity.

Night time puts a different perspective on travel, especially in towns and cities where the traffic signs and signals can be hard to find amongst the background of neon signs, shop windows and hoardings. If it's raining and you are trying to see through a scratched visor or goggles, then even the indicators and brake lights of vehicles nearby can become obscured by the kaleidoscopic effect of abrasions and raindrops. This can be exacerbated by oil smears on the outside and condensation on the inside of your visor. Travelling with the visor up will help at low speeds but soft little raindrops become hard and painful as your speed increases. Having to squint through tearful and bloodshot eyes will not be much of an improvement, so it is worth getting a good visor or pair of goggles and looking after them.

Headlights on main beam or badly aligned through misuse or overloading can be troublesome by day or night. It is difficult to see past the headlights of on-coming vehicles to discover what they belong to. Is it a lorry or just two solo motor bikes side by side? A single light is probably a solo motorcycle but it could be a car with a damaged headlight. Can you judge if the lights are stationary or just moving slowly? Speed assessment and judgement of distance is more difficult at night, especially in unlit areas where nearly all the information available is provided from your own and the oncoming headlight beams. The light intensity is minimal compared to what the eye would normally scan at the same spot during daylight hours. No matter how experienced you are, you can still make misjudgements.

If when looking up the street from a side turning you decide that the on-coming lights are far enough away for you to turn out ahead of them, only to find out you are wrong, then try to minimise the mistake by accelerating hard to reduce the amount of braking the vehicle has to do. Pull over or off to give the motorist as much room for manoeuvre as possible. Accept as gracefully as you can their likely rebukes because the roles could be reversed in the future. Turning out across has fewer alternative strategies. Brake hard, so there is room around the front of you, or accelerate to give room around the back, but do not freeze in the centre of the street or you could end up as a bonnet mascot.

Teaming rain gathers into puddles which grow in size until they become a flood. Water reduces tyre-grip, plus the amount of power which can be used for acceleration and cornering. Braking distances are also considerably increased. Even when travelling at fairly modest speeds, meeting a stream or puddle of H_2O can make your front wheel take up water ski-ing; known to those that survive it as acquaplaning.

This levitation of tread means you lack the ability to steer, which is exactly what you do not need when approaching a corner. As with driving on ice, do not indulge in sudden movements. Keep the machine as vertical as possible, wind off the power and be gentle on the rear brake until you feel that rolling resistance again as the front tyre returns to *terra firma*. Apply the front brake and recover the ability to steer – with luck, before you need to turn!

Ice like water on oily surfaces as found on roundabouts, motorway exits, arterial roads, bus stops and garage forecourts requires mere mortals to a slow to a steady and gentle pace in the knowledge that hitting tarmac hurts – and more so as your velocity increases. At slow speeds on snow and ice, leave your legs dangling to act as stabilisers, riding in or close to the gutter to find some grip in the unimpacted snow or unpolished ice. Thus when the time comes when you take a closer look at the wonders that nature has bestowed, the chances are you will be able to fall towards and onto the verge or kerb, rather than into the road and under the wheels of your average under-skilled tin top pilot.

Fog or mist requires caution – not just for the conditions you are riding in and through, but because motorists tend to pack up behind the slowest and most incompetent wally. It only takes a short time for the queue to lengthen to such extent that there is little chance of overtaking. In their frustration, however, some motorists may try and if you cannot see more than five cars ahead, and he has got past twice that amount, then it's down to luck as to whether he makes it. Luck is a very unreliable commodity that we all need at some time, but it will not necessarily be there when you need it most. So what if it is you coming the other way down the centre white line. In these conditions the risk of a collision is not as high as driving on the kerb, with its parked cars, unlit skips, junctions and lay-bys, but the impact will be far more devastating. The compromise is to be towards the middle of your side, whilst still being able to see the centre line. This also gives you the best chance if there is any stationary vehicle waiting to turn off either to the left or right. At night time these problems are compounded by reflective glare from your headlight, and even greater time/distance distortion. If you are on strange streets there is a good chance of becoming disorientated as well.

5

WHO TO LOOK FOR

Milk floats going out with a load and coming back in with batteries flat. They use all of the street, for parking, left, right and centre. Watch out for the operator who can step out either side of the cab.

Invalid cars There are fewer trikes around than there used to be. Life has not been too kind to the drivers of these single seat, under powered, overloaded glassfibre boxes, so do not add to his grief.

Learner drivers One of the great causes of street aggro are thick skinned twits and nervous novices doing their best to bring the traffic to a halt. There should be a two-part driving test so that the basics of car control can be learnt before novices have to tackle street law.

Royal Mail Little red delivery vans with short, sharp, jerky movements which park on yellow lines near Post Boxes and Post Offices.

Dustbin/refuse collectors Recognised by their slow, hesitant crawl up the middle of any street. Two or three operatives, found up to 50 yards in any direction around the truck, will reappear burdened with bags and bins. They unnaturally assume that it's you who will take the avoiding action when they suddenly appear in your path.

Hearses Funeral corteges drive as slowly as in the days when the floral tributes were carried on the roof and the whole ensemble drawn by horses. A couple of official undertakers' motors follow the hearse along with the mourners in everyday civilian cars (their numbers depending on the popularity of the deceased). The result is that the traffic is going to go pretty slowly for the next few miles. On the return from the business of planting they are not any speedier.

Farm Machinery Tractors are the main hassle in this category, distributing large lumps of mud, and hauling insecure loads on antediluvian trailers bereft of brake lights, lights and indicators. Trailers can frequently be encountered around blind bends in a stationary position while the driver opens or closes a gate. Ploughs mounted on a tractor and doubling its length will fill all the street when turning.

Taxis, inner city Not to be confused with their country cousins who are private citizens masquerading as such. Have good car control and very bad road manners.

Caravan Towers An unusual fetish of the middle classes, too posh for B and B's and cannot afford hotels. They are the most likely cause of summertime queues and are especially pig-headed in convoy when they refuse to pull over to dissipate the tail-back.

Livestock and Horse Boxes Cattle trucks in the hands of the farming fraternity loiter with no idea of what is going on around them. Horse boxes are driven by horse riders, an aggressive and volatile hoard that are without courtesy or consideration for others. Can be erratic drivers if they visited the champagne tent after a result at a race meeting.

Buses Not to be confused with coaches, range in size from the 70 plus seat double decker down to 12 plus seat van-based minis.

The bigger the bus, the better the driver but in towns and cities they are running to unrealistic schedules, so if you do not give way, then they will make a way. Bus stops and lay-bys get parked on, so the drivers will double park or the nearest patch of vacant pavement will be utilised for letting off passengers. So, go careful up the inside of stationary buses – you might get stood on by alighting passengers.

Coaches Come in the same range of sizes as buses, but travel longer distances with fewer stops and at higher speeds to deposit their load *en masse* at some scenic wonder, sports event or seaside town. Rubber-necking tourists are not necessarily native to our shores or ways, but standard bikers' gestures are known world-wide and can help get your point of view over. PSV's (passenger service vehicles) are legally able to use the outside overtaking lane of a three-lane motorway, and do at speeds faster than most 250 cc bikes. This causes great air turbulence as they overtake.

Trucks The world's wheels of commerce, for which the streets we use were built, so do not bitch, for without them you could be naked and hungry. The bigger the truck, the harder the test and the greater the skill. Not all trucks are driven by professional drivers. Keep a sharp eye out for 'rental vans', for anybody who has a full car licence can drive a vehicle weighing up to 7½ tons. Commercial vehicle owners and drivers suffer even greater hassles than bikers! And they are never on the road for pleasure.

Wide Loads Normally have jam butties with chequered heads aboard front and rear, with all candles glowing. These will get up-tight if you get between them and their load.

Blue/Green/Orange Flashing Lights: Orange indicate recovery maintenance vehicles, hedge trimmers and Council workers. Not always on at the right time, but best to heed in any event. **Green** is for doctor, so allow free and swift passage. **Blue** not all belong to the chequered skull brigade. Ambulances and fire fighting appliances also have them. Definitely give way for the latter pair as they are helping others. If the 'odd lot' have 'twos and blues' on full volume, you must give way.

6

WHEN TO LOOK

The streets are alive to the sound of cars 24 hours a day, with fluctuations in intensity. Big cities have more, little villages less, traffic but both create situations where death or accident may occur.

In the city refuse and garbage collection starts early in the morning, along with street washing and gutter cleaning. On the main drags, as the morning progresses you will have a considerable flow of heavy freight with milk floats and heavily laden service buses collecting drivers for shift-workers buses. Paper boys and girls, like milk floats and dust carts, ricochet about the street with little or no illumination risking head-on collisions in one-way streets. The bigger industrial estates and factories produce their own traffic congestion as the workers arrive to start the day, followed a little later by school traffic mingling with office staff and middle management.

Seven to 10 am is the first traffic peak; the second one comes during lunch hour.

Snack serving pubs do a good trade with office workers, while middle management frequent hotels and restaurants where alcoholic refreshment is also served. Fast food takeaways are packed with school kids and workers loitering in the heavy outfall of litter who often find their way into amusement arcades or betting offices for the remaining minutes of the dinner break.

After this hoard there is a two-hour lull, so to speak, before peak time traffic. It starts with child collection from kindergartens and schools and leads onto early office leavers competing with the elder kids for the public transport. The admin. section will also try to make it out of the car park before the workers' hooter signals the best aggro of the day. Through all this the commercial wheels still have to trundle, delivering and collecting 90 per cent of all products used and consumed. Coaches hauling the tourists to places of picturesque beauty or historic interest add their own particular contribution to the general melee. In addition there is the ubiquitous representative. Reps in total make up 65 per cent of all cars seen between the peak hours. The high mileages they put in every year ensures that they acquire street technique.

On to the evening, and between 7 and 10.30 pm there is normally a sober drive from the home to evening classes, organisations and the clubs, but the majority go to the boozer. Alcohol is the biggest profitable drug for governments and companies in the world, and if you overdrink you can cause harm to yourself and others. Total abstainers in the UK represent only a lowly fraction of the population; the majority have a preference for one or another of the relaxing beverages offered to the public. Tolerance to the quantity imbibed before becoming horizontal in very variable, influenced by such factors as size, sex and regularity. So 10.30 pm to the early morning is a time of low street density but high risk, as the more drink you put away, the slower your reaction to any situation with which you might be confronted, like having to blow into a breathalyser.

Some of our larger towns and cities have an unofficial red light zone. Here you can find an erratic style of driving which has a certain similarity to the progression of a milk float. 'Kerb crawling', as it is called, is not a complete definition as this does not allow for the sudden unanticipated spurt of acceleration as the driver spots the wife, or some one in blue

with shiny buttons; or deceleration when a suitable unsung social worker hoves into view.

Weekends are worse than weekday driving as the pillock ratio soars, with the professional lorry, rep and coach driver being replaced by the incompetent amateur. Amateurs dawdle and display a serious lack of consideration for those who need to use the streets professionally. Take a count at any traffic light junction during the week on the number of vehicles that get

across on the green, and then count again at the weekend. At the same lights, at the same time, fewer drivers get across.

Out from the city at the weekend the traffic density is usually lower, but watch out for weekend tourists observing the beauties of the countryside rather than the road. Traffic flow slows down in the vicinity of signs for historic houses and viewpoints. In particular treat any area around National Trust signs with caution.

7

WHAT TO DO ABOUT THEM

You have already taken the primary step of recognising potential hazards on the road. Normally you will spend over 80 per cent of your miles on known streets in your locality. So it is logical to assume you are at greatest risk driving in your local area. Get an A–Z street map or an Ordnance Survey, or both, if possible, and nail them to a wall in the bedroom or garage. If you are a sociable fellow your local bikers club room wall is the best bet because the more bikers that participate in the exercise, the quicker the build-up of grief-saving knowledge. Indicate on the map holes, road works and their progress, debris, latest diesel spillages, loiter points for the Plod and known gestapo harrassment spots plus known radar/Vascar/speed traps.

Once your map has its covering of marking pins, seek out alternative routes and check their feasibility. While you are out and about target location of the speed traps, whose positioning can be gathered from the local rag's Court reports. As the police are in action for three to four hours at a time, its possible sometimes to see how they hide and operate the speed traps. The appliance is located near an unmarked vehicle. The officer of the law will sit with his chequered cap off to lessen the chance of being detected, his task is to radio a marked vehicle further on to do the pull – normally in a layby, bus stop or side street. Now, if you are pulled over and you might have been breaking the law and you do nothing but just stand there cogi-

tating on whether it was the indoctrination that turned him into an arse or whether he joined because he already was one, he will get twitchy within a few minutes. A few minutes more and you will have threats hurled at you to get going, pronto. Do not argue, it is a complete waste of time and will not help your case if you are really out of order. Just clock their faces and number so you can build up a dossier on who is most eligible for the bastard of the year award and be able to recognise them, even out of uniform.

The most important piece of information, however, is the registered number on the car, along with make, model and colour. It will help speed up your collection of evil numbers by doing a regular recce of the local nick on, say, four times a week over an eight week period. Note the number on all plain cars you can. Usually leave out those over five years old. The extra aerials used to be a dead give-away but are no longer due to the increasing use of cellular telephones and CB. The picture that builds up over the years of the *modus operandi* of the chequered skull skum in your locality will also help you recognise likely

ambush sites when on travels in areas less well known to you.

Carrying the theme of recognition a bit further, but on a broader band, the ability to recognise vehicle makes and models will give you some idea of their performance potential and the likely performance needed to out drag them at the lights, successfully execute an overtaking maneuvre with them coming at you, or pull out first from a junction. This all ties in with the allocation of points you give on your 'Pillock Ratio Chart'.

Picture yourself coming up behind a Volvo who's behind a laden eight-legger. It will be tucked right up its rear. The Volvo has got more performance than your bike, but the pilot is unlikely to be an enthusiastic street competitor. Around the right hand bend there may be a straight so back off, change down so you can accelerate up to your optimum speed before having to pull out to overtake. As you make the cut in to the bend, give a look up the inside and see if you can check that the street ahead looks clear ready for the slingshot to pass the opposition. It's also worth keeping an eye on the trucker's candles as it is likely he will give the left indicator a couple of flashes to indicate that in his opinion there is no chance to overtake. The right indicator flashing means you should stay your ground.

Unlike the trucker, the Volvo pilot in his armour plated tank cares little of what is going on around him. Unable to progress with his driving skills, he has opted for this upmarket steel cocoon so he can carry on living while maiming others about him. So when you start exiting the bend, going from verge to white lines, flash your lights as you pass his rear view mirror and again when you are in his door mirror. Even this does not guarantee that he will not pull out as you try to pass him. Do not try and run wide until you have eyeballed the blind spot that was left when you looked up the inside of the vehicles on the bend. For other traffic from turnings, driveways and laybys on the right could appear in that blind spot after the truck had passed and signalled it was clear. It is better, if you have cocked it up, to

rub the paint of the Volvo than to be a bonnet mascot on the on-coming vehicle.

Back to the story: no one in the blind spot and your slingshot manoeuvre is well under way when you spot an on-coming car. Depending on whether it is a Renault 4 or a Ferrari 308, you either brake and pull back or keep it well wound on, if necessary crouching to gain some extra speed. It could be a version of the Ford Escort, but which one – the 1100 slug or the XR3i rocket ship? If in doubt, chicken out.

Building up a picture of the street opposition can play a big part in lending a smoother flow and style to your combat riding.

Take a hypothetical case of approaching a roundabout. You are checking your right when you notice a van that is just joining from the next road up. Is it the local builder's tired Transit or an express parcel delivery Sherpa complete with young hotshoe pilot? Again, it is the difference between braking and acceler-

ation. By being able to discern what the vehicle is, and its ability to perform, you can reduce the time wasted in waiting for the pillock to react and make a smoother, faster, passage. This can be observed any day of the week at your local idiot roundabout where you can see three or four cars facing each other, each one waiting for the one on his right to move off. If, having filtered through the jam you find this situation confronting you, check the pillock on your right, using the above criteria and also the car you are alongside. If you get it wrong, you could end up clobbered by them both. So be positive. A rapid assimilation is called for. Who is the opposition looking at – you or each other? What is the performance differential? Is it in your favour, and is it likely to be used? What is the street condition? Remember, they have difficulty in seeing you on a good day, so what hope have you got on a dirty wet evening?

8

PRACTICAL MIND GAMES AND MENTAL DEVIATION

In your daily commuting, you will recognise certain places as being particularly hazardous for bikers. Play through the cranium a 'what if' scenario, what if, on this blind brow, you meet a vehicle coming at you; the driver having decided that he could not wait behind that milk float a moment longer. Besides, when he did the same thing yesterday, there was not anything coming then!

Well, today, maybe it is your turn to meet a pillock. What would you do –what *could* you do? Check for a free space on the left? A bus stop, lay-by, side street? You may not have enough room to stop, but your impact speed on a stationary object will be a lot less than colliding with the on-coming vehicle whose velocity, if added to your's, will inflict grievous bodily harm on contact. (Add your 20 mph to his 20 mph = 40 mph equals SPLAT.) If the left is no go, you might have space on your right, but could you get there before the pillock gets you? In choosing the lesser of two evils you might end up with a buggered bike, a buckled body and having to cope with a bloody minded owner of whatever it was you *apparently* attacked. If you are unlucky and nobody comes forth to corroborate the facts, the police will probably nick you for dangerous or careless driving. Later, as you lay in your hopsital bed perusing that registered hate mail, you may feel that life ain't fair. You will not be the first or the last to have noticed that fact. The alternative

scenario of a head-on would legally put you in the right, but it would probably be a posthumous victory.

What if neither side offers an option, if for instance you are going over a narrow bridge without a footpath, or one which is too high to mount? Then go for the slower vehicle which is being overtaken because its braking distance will be a lot shorter than the speeding pillock's. But this is not all you can do. A technique used in the past in the lower speed impact range is that of braking right up to a yard or so away and then releasing the brakes. By pulling a wheelie, the bike's underside impacts with the vehicle. Now, if you are riding a Z1300 the next thing that happens is going to hurt a lot more than if you're on a furious 50. Having had all the air pushed out of you by meeting the tank with your chest, the ungrateful lump of iron will fall on you as it rebounds off the offending vehicle – or you may have practised longer, in which case you might be able to deflect the bike away from you.

Sumping an oncoming vehicle can reduce your chance of being propelled into, or over and into something else travelling at even greater speed. The rebound speed will be a lot less than your impact speed and you will probably also reduce the structural damage to the bike.

Some racers, thrown onto the track at 100 mph, get up and walk away with nothing more serious than skin burns and gravel rash. But the likelihood of finding a quarter-mile of very smooth, unimpeded blacktop is remote. In all probability it will have kerbs, cars, road signs, light standards, post boxes, telephone kiosks, keep left bollards and road works. Any one of these, even if hit at 10 mph, can break up your internal chassis.

In the wet, cadence braking is particularly useful. By repeatedly applying the brakes and releasing them before the wheels lock braking distances are reduced and the ability to steer retained.

Having reduced the speed as much as possible, the 180° burn is another option to consider when faced with an oncoming vehicle. The sequence goes like this: clutch in, front brake off, rear brake hard on resulting in rear wheel lock.

Apply left lock on the bars if the safer space is on your right, or right lock if usable area is on left. The rear wheel should now proceed to overtake the front. Taking care not to let the rear drop as it gets sideways on, return the bars to the straight-ahead position, release the clutch on enough throttle to pull the bike upright and overcome the pre-manoeuvre forward momentum.

Applying techniques like these without first practising at slow speeds on soft soil with a rat bike and dead cars and getting away with it is the work of a genius. Rat bike and some soft soil will probably give you a better return on your money than time spent on anything else in your biking life. They will enable you to explore and develop alternative strategies for incidents that would not ordinarily leave you time to think and act. Filtering up the inside of traffic, passing parked cars, a door starts open-ing as you pass. Could you boot it shut again without loosing your balance, or fend off a pedestrian who has just stepped from the pavement into your side without ending up in a mess? What are the limits to riding with a flat tyre on sand, gravel or grass? Can you let the bike down so it goes away from you, enabling you to decelerate quicker than the combined mass? The bike has a smaller surface area in contact with the ground, and with you on it, it will take longer to loose momentum. With practice, sliding on your back, keeping feet first, head up, and looking over toenails, you will be able to minimise your impact on stationary objects. It's certainly more effective than curling up in a ball and taking a chance on what part gets clobbered first.

If you club together with one or more compatriots, with a couple of tenners each to do the rounds of your dealers and breakers in your area, you are bound to be offered some half decent wreck or write-off. Go for the bigger capacity machine, even when clapped, because this will still produce a modicum of reasonable performance and be a prelude to the day that you can afford and legally run such capacity on the streets.

Storage and transport are the most likely problems as running costs and maintenance are quite minimal. Storage on site – such as on a farm, sandpit or tip – reduces the temptation to illegally ride the bike on public roads. Even if pleading with kith and kin has been to no avail – they have better things to do than hump lumps of oily metal in and out of the family transport – don't give those chequered skull heavies an opportunity to cause you grief. As a biker, you are not likely to be the flavour of the month in your street and possibly any neighbour will be only too pleased to shop you, especially those involved in the police sneak scheme called Neighbourhood Watch. Some even have stickers in their windows declaring their intentions.

Put a wheel to the street on a bike in unroadworthy condition, with no insurance, tax, MOT or licence and you could find yourself in front of three police toadies who would probably volunteer for the job of hangperson should some Conservatives get the death penalty reinstated. So, if you cannot ride it, or push it, what can you do?

Legally, your machine needs to be carried. A trailer, a pair of skateboards or roller skate frames can suffice if you do not have to travel far. Legally, what constitutes a motor vehicle is a vague area open to the Plod's interpretation. A motor vehicle is not a motor vehicle if its motor does not work. Removing the chain and sparking plugs should be legal, but nothing less than taking out the engine and transporting it at a separate time can guarantee the acceptance of the meaning 'non-functional.' The police can nick you for obstruction, loitering with intent, or suspicion of stolen property. Do not give in. The effort to keep a rat rolling is far too rewarding, and gives satisfaction far in excess of the effort expended.

If driving with a passenger is a new experience for you, or both of you, try and refrain from demonstrating your prowess until you have sussed out the effects on the bike's handling and performance.

Give basic instructions on what you require of the passenger before mounting the machine. It's up to you to put the pillion's footrests down (he may not know how). Ignite the wick or give the kick start a prodding, and only when firmly seated, then give him the nod to mount. Mounting from the nearside, your passenger should place his left foot on the footrest and hand on your shoulder, slinging his right leg over the seat and onto the offside peg and lowering himself onto the bike. This system is better than the unpremeditated arrival of 100 plus pounds on the bike whilst the biker is trying to find his own balance.

It is easier to control the bike if the pillion leans on you rather than sitting upright.

So even if your passenger is inattentive or travelling with their eyes shut, their mass (most of which is the wrong side of

the rear wheel spindle) will still follow your movements, no matter how rapid. Sitting away from you means that an instinctive reaction on your part will probably not prompt an immediate response from your pillion and this delay can lead to that famous bikers' dance for two, 'rear end wallow.' A secondary benefit is lower drag and turbulance and a better chance to recover balance if the pilot suddenly decides to economise on tyres and pulls a wheelie without warning of his intentions.

Carrying this extra mass is unlikely to improve the bike's

handling and certainly will not help in braking or acceleration as this extra weight, on or behind the rear spindle, increase the chances of your popping wheelies under acceleration. Under heavy braking your passenger may well display a tendency to climb up your back, thus increasing the load on your arms and crutch. As if that is not enough, there is all the paraphernalia of touring and camping to stow in the top box and panniers, with perhaps even a rucksack added for full measure. All this extra weight at the rear will require an increase in your tyre pressures and a winding-up of the spring and damper system. The bike handbook will usually contain sufficient information on tyre pressures and suspension ratings but if you are not on the original brand of rubber you will probably have to experiment a little to find the optimum settings.

A secure tank bag has many advantages. The bike's handling is largely unaffected as the load is inside the wheel base. The bag also helps to stop you sliding up the tank under heavy braking. Many bags feature a transparent map pocket on top with coin pockets on the side for toll money. Bags can usually be quickly released to provide instant access to the filler cap, and, if you are so inclined, they can be used as walk-about handbags.

9

LAW AND USEFUL FACTS

There are thousands of laws relating to motoring, with more being added all the time and very few being deleted. As a motorcylist you have less than a 50 per cent chance of keeping off the police computer for law infringement. Stationary offences such as illegal parking are usually dealt with by traffic wardens. If you are nicked by the bullies in blue, it will probably be for a driving offence. They have probably been following you or you have passed them whilst exceeding the legal speed limit. The latter is easy to do in bad conditions at night or if the police car is unmarked. They next try to get your attention usually with blue flashing lights, two-tone horns and hand waving. This should be interpreted as a demand for you to pull over and stop. You have not much of an option because once they have your registration number they also have access to your name, address, age, sex and any previous offences. In city traffic, if they are in a car and have not been able to get alongside, you can take advantage of the bike's smaller size to filter between the traffic and make a clean getaway. If you are apprehended, you can always claim that you did not see them signalling for you to stop.

On motorways, if your bike is a better performer you could out-run them, but this causes them to become twice as can-tankerous as it indicates contempt and a lack of trepidation for their law and uniform. It also raises the stakes on what sort of summons you will receive.

When yo are pulled in, certain demands will be made such as

'Stop the engine . . . Get off the bike . . . Let's see your documents' and 'Breathe into this box.' They will call you sir or madam and make it sound like an insult. If it was a day-glo tip top that pulled you in, then you will find yourself up against a pair of chequered skulls. While one is trying to get you to incriminate yourself (which if you do, he will take down and read out in Court, making you sound a bigger twit than you really are), the other is looking for any mechanical defect or

fault on the machine, and checking with the computers to see if your recorded details match those given by you. If your documents are not on your person, you have a few days to produce them at the nick of your choice. You will also be given a ticket which will detail any offences you may have committed. And should you be over the alcohol limit, it is a ride in the day-glo, a piss and a prick at the nick and maybe a night in the cells.

Later, you will be served with a detailed summons telling you when and where to appear in court. This would normally be at a local Magistrates/Justice of the Peace Court but before pleading guilty by form, or appearing in court, check with the Citizens Advice Bureaux about solicitors on the cheap advice scheme. If you feel that the prosecution is coming on really heavy, go straight to a legal eagle. He is a professional pleaser of magistrates, many of whom are unpaid amateurs from the same social strata as the upper-middle echelons as the top constabulary, whom they believe can do no wrong, this means that the police can and have got away with murder.

If you are not expecting justice, then you will not be disappointed. Just try and minimise the humiliating harassment and hassle they try to put you through and ignore the contempt with which you are treated. Do not get dispondent as you stand in the dock receiving your sentence before that bunch of old gestapo groupies. Be philosophical – you can afford to sacrifice one day from the rich panoply of your life.

10

ENGINEERING CONCEPTS AND APPLICATION

Monotrack vehicles cannot stay upright when stationary, so retractable props such as side and centre stands have to be used. Once under way, even at walking pace, the machine becomes balanced and retains stability. The faster the wheels rotate, the more stable the line of travel and the more force required for deflection. This affect can be felt if you spin a bicycle wheel while holding the spindle with arm outstretched. Turning the spindle to the left results in a sharp tilt of the wheel in the opposite direction. However, banking the spindle to the left results in the wheel turning smoothly in the same direction. These are examples of gyroscopic progressions. Centrifugal and gravitational forces also come into the equation as you corner, and it is the right mix that makes for the magic of biking.

To achieve a left turn, pull down on the left bar. As the gyroscopic procession comes into effect, push forward on the same bar – balacing it against the throttle – to hold the required radius. Then, coming out of the turn, accelerate to increase the wheels' gyro effect which pulls the bike back on the vertical. Nice one, Newton.

At slow speeds you steer the bike with lots of lock and little lean. As speed increases the opposite happens – lots of lean with little lock. In effect, you are balancing velocity against gravitational pull: a corner taken at 60 mph at 40° of dangle is smooth, but the same corner, taken at 40° of dangle at 5 mph would have you on your ear.

Tank slappers, a long-established topic for tall stories and sagas, are the result of the gyroscopic procession being put out of syncro by a sudden deflection of the steering due to clipping some street debris or dropping into a pothole. A tank slapper is more likely to happen to some machines than others – more on a Honda Goldwing, less on a Ducati – more on a Kawasaki Z1300 and less on a Fizzy. The heavier a bike is, the greater the chance of tank slapping. Ultimately, it depends on how far the

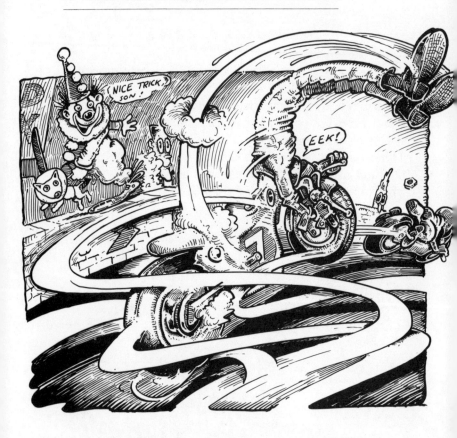

weight is distributed from the bike's centre line – a line extending from the biker's head down to the rear tyre's contact point with the road surface.

If you could watch it in slow motion from above, you would see the head set swinging to and fro across the centre line causing the front forks to turn in the opposite direction. The mass picks up momentum very quickly, producing more energy than can be contained by a mere mortal. A shit stirring, brain draining, knee knocking experience! So what can you do? Shut the throttle. Do not try and ride through it. The faster you go, the quicker the oscillation. In theory, if you can go quick enough this will resynchronise the gyros, but it's unlikely you will have the necessary performance or street experience. The faster you go, the harder you fall, so shut the throttle, apply the rear brake *only*, get as much weight as possible over the front by laying over the head set (it reduces the oscillating mass), and keep your eyes open to look for soft landing places. You may need them.

Having survived and regained composure, check for the reason. It could be a deflating tyre, shagged swing arm bushes, knackered forks or wheel bearings. If the cause of your *contretemps* was a hole or debris, make a formal complaint at the local nick.

High siding is another way to meet *terra firma*. It is similar in many ways to the tank slapper and even more spectacular. The back end breaks away; you turn into the skid, containing it but reapplying too much power with the result that the back end pushes the head set to the opposite side. This causes the bike to immediately de-accelerate, however the rider's momentum has increased to such a velocity that he can be catapulted over the bars as the head set swings to the side the skid occurred on. Some of the best examples of this phenomenon can be seen on televised Grand Prix motocycle racing.

CONTINENTAL MAYHEM

It is easier than you think, and probably cheaper, to get to the Continent. There are plenty of professional organised tours by 'one-make' clubs. Some members of the travel trade specialise in bikers and you can find some splendid offers in the more reputable motor cycling monthlies to enable you to gain some experience of Europeans and their habits.

Doing for yourself will probably not be any cheaper, but it can offer a greater sense of adventure with more entertaining sagas to be told on returning to Albion. You will need a passport – a one year version covering European countries can be obtained from main Post Offices. Also necessary is a Green Card from your insurance company or broker and an EIII European health ticket from your Social Security office. The latter is particularly useful if you make it to Spain. You will also need an International Licence, a few pounds, a couple of extra passport snaps, UK licence, GB sticker and log book. The Automobile Association offers a Five Star Continental Get You and Yours Home insurance which is nice and comforting if you can afford it.

If spontaneity is what you are after, then armed with tent and sleeping bag, just power down to a port opposite the country you are aiming for, purchase a standby ticket and depending on season, strikes or luck, they will pack you aboard sooner or later.

Watch out for the slippery polished steel ramp, lethal when damp and even more exciting if you have imbibed some fer-

mented beverages to while away the time. Yesterday's dinner is likely to begin to make itself felt when you get underway, so a couple of polythene bags or bin liners will save that mad sprint to the overcrowded urinal (or in nautical terminology, 'the heads.') After that Technicolor yawn into your very own personal puke bag, you deserve brownie points if you remember to tape the neck before depositing it in front of your fellow passengers as a means of stimulating flagging dialogue.

Having disembarked and waved your passport at the relevant officialdom, the first and probably the most lasting impression you will receive is that the rest of the EEC is definitely out of step, positively demanding that you drive on the right. This is not too difficult to achieve as long as you are awake and driving with other traffic. It is when you arrive at a junction that the

problems arise, especially when joining a dual carriageway or roundabout with a sign saying '*Vous n'avez pas la priorité*' or '*Cédez le passage*', meaning traffic on roundabout has priority. If there are no signs, traffic entering the roundabout has priority.

And in the more ancient French towns, especially, beware of the notorious '*Priorité à Droite*'. This means a vehicle entering from a side street can, without warning, enter a more major road without having to give warning. If you get hit by a 2CV you will not have a leg to stand on – physically or legally. The French also have more drunks on the road than any other EEC country.

Continental Porkies are no more lenient than our home grown variety. If they see you doing a no-no, they will dip into your pocket and hit you with a spot fine. Make sure you know what is necessary to be legal in whichever country you are – for example, in France you will be done for not driving on dipped beam during the day.

Beware also, that many European police are not police in the sense we Britons understand the word. The top guns in most cases are really soldiers and apart from being armed they are also permitted to use violent methods which would cause an eyebrow to be raised on the Milwall Football Club terraces.

12

BODGES AND DODGES

Murphy's Law as applied to motorcycling is that if it can go wrong it will, and at the most inconvenient time and place. Although you may not be able to stop it happening, you can reduce the amount of aggro it causes by using what you have got in the tool kit and a little lateral thinking.

A selection of spanners suitable in size for the nuts and bolts on your machine, screwdrivers (plain and posidrive) a set of molegrips and a roll of gaffer tape make up a basic kit. Spares that should always be carried but somehow seldom are, include bulbs for front and rear lights, complete clutch and throttle cables or inner with screw-on nipples, and fuses or a portion of tin foil. Indispensable is a puncture repair kit, spare tube (or a tin of bung up and inflate), tyre levers, spare chain links, spark plugs – especially on 'strokers – and perhaps a metre or so of syphoning tube.

Now, what to do when the machine ceases to function and you are not in possession of the replacement component and your AA/RAC Relay Membership has lapsed, or never existed in the first place?

Well, depending on the degree of desperation, here are some suggestions for the more common calamities.

Punctures You can walk beside the machine, slipping the clutch where necessary, with engine ticking over in first gear. This saves the sweat of pushing. If you do not mind buggering up the tube, sit on and trickle home.

Loss of split link This absence may be redeemed by acquiring a length of fencing wire, bending it into a 'U' of the same pitch as the chain, passing it through the chain ends and twisting together the protruding length. Gently on the throttle and it will probably get you a mile or two.

No spark situation A malfunctioning kill switch can some-times be rectified by taking length of redundant wiring from the harness (such as the front side light, near side indicator or rear brake light), stripping the ends and connecting the battery directly to the coil.

Points These are always a hassle. If, when peering in, you notice that the heel has worn or broken off so it is no longer opening, try bending the points arms, or removing the screw from the adjustment slot, relying on just the fulcrum screw to hold the plate when it has been repositioned to make a gap. If you cannot find the points, do not worry, not all machines have them.

Hole in the piston If you have the spanners to remove the head and barrel, this problem can be temporarily overcome. Remove nut and bolt securing the mudguard stay or clamp, tilt the piston, pass the bolt up through it and place on washer and nut. Tighten, then bruise the remaining thread to reduce the possibility of the nut coming undone. But note, do not remove any important nut and bolt for this job.

Breaking cables, detached nipples The molegrips are useful for clamping the inner cable to the handlebar lever. If necessary, unwind the outer to give you enough length – and use the kill switch instead of clutch when changing gear. The clutch lever should only be used for standing starts. If the outer throttle cable is taped onto the outside of its housing and the inner taped to the grip, sufficient actuation can be gently applied to get you mobile again.

Juice donor You need a way of transferring the necessary supply of petrol. If a tube is available, a car petrol tank can be made to liberate some of its contents. You can check to see if there is any petrol in there by inserting the tube and blowing: if there's any petrol in there, you will hear a bubbling sound or see the depth on the withdrawn tube as a wet tide mark.

Next problem, if you are not very careful, will be a strong mouthwash of four-star. Petrol can also be made to syphon by blowing into the tank. If you wrap a rag, scarf or hanky, around the syphon tube and filler neck, leaving just a small aperture to blow through depending on how full it is and the breather is in the neck, a couple of good puffs and it will be flowing along as the hose exit is lower than the fuel level; it will siphon until it's empty. Next problem – what to put the petrol in. Containers such as milk bottles, coke cans, milk cartons, polythene bags, etc., are normally available within a few minutes' walk in your average urban environment but out there in the sticks there is shortage of litter, so remove a side cover/indicator or rear light lens and put fingers or tape over the holes. May not be the swiftest way to transfer fuel, but it is better than walking. If someone stops, it will more than likely be another biker, so

remove the fuel pipe off his carb and use the petrol tap for flow control. However, be careful. Many plastic containers will dissolve in petrol. And make certain there are no naked flames, sparks or cigarettes around when playing with fuel.

Bulb failure If it is the rear light it is possible to adjust, bend or tie the brake light switch so that the brake light stays on. When the dip filament goes, it is only courteous to move the headlight to bring the beam down to the dipped length, or if that is not possible, tape up or put your glove over the top half of the headlight.

Electrical failure because of blown fuse can be remedied by changing from one to another circuit that is less critical, for example, horn, indicators, etc. If that one also blows, wrap a piece of tinfoil around it and re-insert. The insides of cigarette cartons are good, but any metal object will do – bolt, fence wire etc. Or, if you are feeling technical, take out a redundant wire – say the side light – strip off the outer and use a single strand by wrapping it around fuse mounting clips. Then keep a watch out for the smell of smouldering wiring and black clouds of smoke, or you may have an insurance write-off under your bum.

Be Warned! Like all bodges, the temporary expedient may cause greater problems than it solves – balance your need against the risks involved.

13

WHO TO BE INVOLVED WITH

**British Motorcyclists Federation
Motorcycle Action Group**

BMF and MAG are essential for keeping you informed about government legislation and to enable the voice of motorcycling to be heard above the babble of Parliament. It is necessary to

join these two groups, not only to retard the malicious activities of your local MP, but to reduce the chances of bikers being represented by extreme elements. Those in the BMF are working hard to join the establishment, no matter what it costs, and MAG have members who are working to dismantle the establishment.

So which ever one is your preference, join the other as well for a more balanced and unified force with which to fight against the infringements of your liberty.

One-Make Clubs

Amongst others, Honda, Kawasaki, Suzuki, Yamaha, Vincent, BSA, and Norton have their own dedicated clubs. One-make clubs are normally affiliated to the BMF and have a fund of information not generally found in the handbooks and may offer a small discount off parts from the dealers.

And do not forget the international clubs for women only:

WIMA. (Womens International Motorcycle Association) Secretary: Widgey Thorpe, School House, Sudbrook, Gwent, NP6 4SY

There is something for everybody in biking.

Christian Riders, Trial Riders Fellowship and **National Chopper** are just some of the clubs that cater for the spirit as well as the machine.

Officially blessed training schemes include the following:

British Motorcyclists Federation Rider Training Schemes,
  PO Box 2, Uckfield, East Sussex TN22 3ND

National Motorway Star Rider Training Scheme
  239/11 Coventry Road, Sheldon, Birmingham B26 3PB

ROSPA Motorcycle Training Scheme
  Cannon House, The Priory, Queensway, Birmingham B4 6BS

And be alert for your local groupings. Often these meet at pubs where the landlord has an enlightened attitude towards bikes, bikers and biking. The very worst that will come of joining one of these gatherings is a good time.

Automobile Association
Royal Automobile Club

The AA and the RAC will get you home in cases of calamity and also help with route planning and Continental sorties. You cannot expect instant roadside service for the price but we have been pleasantly surprised by the quality of the patrolmen, especially considering their low pay and inconvenient hours.

14

MIND EXPANDING READING

For a more in-depth look at some of the topics covered in this book, these publications are available at your local library. If they are not in stock, libraries will usually acquire them for you. Or, if you are flushed with the readies, purchase from a good bookshop. Many are willing to order if they are not in stock of a particular title.

Motorcycle Chassis Design   Vic Willoughby & Tony Foale (Osprey)

Second Lap   Paul Blezzard & John Taylor
All the information on trail parks

Whatever Happened to the British Motorcycle Industry?
Bert Hopwood
Insight to national calamity

FF Information Pack   Royce Creasy
Goes on from where Willoughby & Foale leave off
Available from 31 Gratitude Road, Greenbank, Bristol

Aerodynamics of Road Vehicles   Wold–Heinrich Hucho
Title says it all

Zen and the Art of Motorcycle Maintenance   Robert Pirsig

Jupiters Travels   Ted Simon
The above two books provide an insight into other bikers' visions and perception. Mind games extraordinaire.

Hitch Hiders Guide to Europe   Ken Walsh
For those not overwhelmed with large amounts of disposable cash, this book and others like it help us get the most out of what we have got .

Kitchens Road Transport Law Year Book
A summary of the legislation affecting construction equipment and use of motor vehicles

The Driving Test   Brian Stratton
The official jargon and system explained

For 'one-make' histories   Roy Bacon (most available from Osprey)
Mainly British bikes but is making a start on the Nippon mob

Police Gazette
A weekly periodical providing an insight into how they see themselves and you.